·TESCO· COOKERY· COLLECTION·

MICROWAVE COOKING

TESCO

ACKNOWLEDGEMENTS

The publishers would like to thank the following companies
for their kindness in providing materials and equipment
used in the photography for this book:
David Mellor, 26 James Street, London WC2;
Elizabeth David, 46 Bourne Street, London SW1;
Harrods and Way In, Knightsbridge, London SW1;
Sharp Electronics (UK); Thorpac Group plc;
Toshiba UK Ltd; Lakeland Plastics

We would also like to thank the following who
were concerned in the preparation of the book.

Series Art Director Pedro Prá-Lopez
Editor Coralie Dorman
Photographer Philip Dowell; (pages 13, 24-5, 61, 62-3 Martin Brigdale)
Stylist Lesley Richardson; (pages 13, 24-5, 61, 62-3 Dawn Lane)
Food prepared for photography by Val Barrett (pages 13, 24-5, 61, 62-3 Stella Murphy)

CONTENTS

NOTE

Standard spoon measurements are used in all recipes

1 tablespoon (tbls) = one 15 ml spoon
1 teaspoon (tsp) = one 5 ml spoon
All spoon measures are level

All eggs are sizes 3 or 4 (standard) unless otherwise stated.

For all recipes, quantities are given in both
metric and imperial measures. Follow either set
but not a mixture of both, as they are not interchangeable.

We set up our Consumer Advisory Service in response to the many pleas for information and cooking ideas we received from our customers. It is run by our team of qualified home economists who answer queries, offer practical advice on cookery and the home and give talks and demonstrations on new products and equipment. The resounding success of the service and the continued demand for more and more recipes and information has now prompted us to produce our own special range of Tesco Cookery Books.
Our series starts with 12 books, each one focusing on an area that our customers have shown particular interest in. Each book contains practical background information on the chosen subject and concentrates on a wide selection of carefully tested recipes, each one illustrated in colour.

Microwave Cooking contains an important new area of food preparation, explaining clearly and simply both the principles of microwave cooking and the practical possibilities it offers for today's busy lifestyle. With the help of charts for instant reference and a large number of tasty, uncomplicated recipes from tea-time baking to snacks, suppers and three-course meals you will have to hand all the materials you need to bring the whole range of your cooking skills firmly into the 1980s.
I very much hope you will enjoy looking through the pages which follow, trying out the recipes and above all tasting and enjoying the results. Happy Cooking!

Carey Dennis, senior home economist, Tesco Stores Ltd.

The idea of cooking food by microwaves in a matter of minutes and in ordinary utensils – some even made of paper – is still sufficiently new to surprise and intrigue. More and more people are buying microwave ovens, attracted by their high-tech speed and efficiency coupled with low running costs.

The basic principle behind the microwave oven is a simple one: the food is cooked by the action of the microwaves on its water molecules. The waves cause the molecules to vibrate at enormously high speed, creating frictional heat. As the microwaves are only attracted to water molecules and are absorbed by them, they pass directly through the cooking utensil into the food. Metal is the only substance with which this process does not work, as it reflects the microwaves, making it impossible for them to reach the food.

The microwave oven

The microwave oven is a small appliance, and thus ideal if kitchen space is limited. It is easy to site, for it can be plugged into any conveniently placed 13 amp socket. The power flows into the transformer where it is increased to a very high voltage. The power then passes through the magnetron (the heart of the oven) which converts it to microwaves. The wave stirrer blade, fan or paddle, distributes the microwaves evenly around the oven cavity.

The microwave oven cannot completely replace conventional appliances, as there are some things it just cannot do, like deep-frying or grilling, or boiling eggs (they explode). However today's models are becoming more and more highly developed, offering a wider range of settings which enable a large choice of dishes to be cooked.

Your own household needs will to some extent dictate the size and complexity of the microwave oven you require. Do you want to use it for defrosting and reheating, preparing convenience foods and drinks? Do you plan to use it as a cooking aid, in combination with another cooker, or as your main oven? If the answer to the last question is yes, a model with variable settings, browning elements, shelves and a higher wattage would be a good choice. If your needs are more basic, then you will probably find that a simple oven with just two cooking settings is perfectly adequate.

Extras in a microwave oven

The basic microwave oven consists of a timer, a cooking control, a door opening device and a start control. The timer is divided into minutes. Cooking controls vary quite considerably. A basic model has a **Low** or **Defrost** and a **High** (the same as 'Full Power or Maximum') setting. The controls on more sophisticated models also include keep warm, simmer, medium, bake, roast and reheat. Until recently, it was not really possible to cook the less expensive (and usually less tender) cuts of meats in a microwave because the cooking time was so fast that the meat remained tough. Now, meat cooked on simmer or roast produces very satisfactory results. Some models are fitted with turntables to ensure an even cooking result while others have a pulsator which does the same job.

Food cooked by microwaves does not brown in the conventional way, which is why some of the more sophisticated models are fitted with a browning element. Remember, though, that you will still need your conventional cooker for the grill, and you may find this adequate for browning too.

Wattage

The wattage of the microwave oven will determine how long the food takes to cook. Domestic models vary from 400 to 700 watts. The lower the power rating, the longer the food will take to cook. Most microwave recipes in cooking books are tested in ovens with an output of between 600 and 700 watts.

Microwave

One of the most positive aspects of microwave cooking is that almost any utensil except those made of metal or aluminium foil can be used. China, glass, plastic, wood, basketware and paper dishes are all suitable, though wood and basketware are only suitable for warming, and paper for especially short-term cooking. The microwave gives a whole new dimension to oven-to-table ware, as all the food can be cooked and served in the same dishes.

Do remember that the heat of the food will heat the containers used. Always use oven gloves when removing full containers from the microwave and take especial care when the food has been cooking for more than two or three minutes.

Both absorbent kitchen and greaseproof paper can be used successfully to cover food in the microwave. Waxed paper should not be used because the heat from the food would melt the wax. Cling film is ideal for wrapping as well as covering food, and roasting bags and boil-in-the bag pouches are also suitable. Care should be taken when removing cling film used as a cover as the steam which it generates can easily scald your hands and face. Remove the side furthest away from you first.

Metal dishes or foil containers should *never* be used in the microwave oven, nor should any utensils which have metallic trims or decoration. Metal reflects the microwaves back to the oven walls causing 'arcing' or flashing which would damage the magnetron.

Some manufacturers state that small pieces of foil can be used to prevent burning, for example, the wing and leg tips of chicken, or the cutlet bones in a crown roast. But whenever foil is used to prevent food from overcooking, it should be applied as sparingly as possible. If your oven has a fan or cooling system and paper tends to blow about, the foil must be very carefully secured, to avoid any contact with the oven walls. Always check the manufacturers' instructions very carefully before using foil.

Several ranges of specially developed microware containers are now available and these are well worth the investment if you intend to use your microwave oven frequently and in a big way. Particularly useful is a browning dish or a skillet.

● A selection of the raw ingredients and equipment needed for the finished recipes illustrated on pages 8 and 9

Cooking techniques

Microwaves radiate in a circular pattern rather like the rings on a dartboard round the central bull's-eye, which means there are hot and cold spots in the oven. The food needs to be turned, rearranged and stirred frequently to distribute the heat more evenly. A turntable assists this process.

Food in the microwave often needs to be covered in the same way as in conventional cooking. Some foods will spit or pop during cooking and these should be covered with kitchen paper.

Recipes will state when covering is required otherwise. All foods in a skin, such as potatoes, tomatoes, apples, sausages and kidneys should be pricked with a fork to prevent them exploding.

Standing times

As the food is cooked so quickly it will still retain a great deal of heat after it is taken out of the microwave oven. It should be left to stand to let the heat distribute itself evenly and thus complete the cooking process.

Timing

Timing is crucial in microwave cooking: overcooking will dry out food and make it tough and inedible. The golden rule is to undercook — the food can always be cooked a little longer if necessary. Quantities will also make a difference, because the level of microwave energy remains the same but has to be divided between the increased amount of food: for example, one potato will take 5 minutes to cook but two will take 8 minutes.

From freezer to microwave

The freezer and microwave make a very happy marriage for the busy cook. When reheating ready-made dishes in the microwave, as opposed to the conventional oven, the original texture of the food remains unchanged. Remember not to freeze food in foil dishes, however, as these cannot be used in the microwave. It is also a good idea to undercook made-up dishes slightly before freezing, so that there is no possibility of overcooking during reheating.

Cover any foods with liquid, but dry foods like oven chips should only be covered with kitchen paper. Dishes with gravy can be reheated in shallow containers to cut down the reheating time but be careful not to let the sauce dry out before the meal is properly reheated. Whole joints of meat can be defrosted in the microwave ready for microwave or conventional cooking. Be sure to allow the joint to 'rest' between defrosting and cooking to ensure that it is thoroughly defrosted.

● Lemon curd; Strawberry soufflé; Chocolate cake; Dry spiced lamb chops; Glazed mange-tout; Country-style pâté; Sole in tomato and mushroom sauce

MICROWAVE COOKING TIMES

The recipes in this book were tested on a 600-650 watt microwave cooker. If you have a microwave cooker with higher or lower wattage, please make the following adjustments:

- for a 500 watt microwave cooker *increase* the cooking time by about 20 seconds for every minute that is given

- for a 700 watt microwave cooker *decrease* the cooking time by about 20 seconds for every minute that is given

COOKING TIMES FOR FRESH MEAT, FISH AND VEGETABLES

Food	Setting	Cooking time per 450 g (1 lb)
Beef, boned and rolled	High	6-7 minutes (rare)
		7-8 minutes (medium)
		8½-9 minutes (well-done)
Chicken, whole	High	6-8 minutes
2 pieces	High	3½-5½ minutes
Duck, whole	Medium	9-11 minutes
Lamb joint	Medium	11-13 minutes
Pork joint	Medium	13-15 minutes
Veal joint	Medium	11-12 minutes
Turkey	Medium	11-12 minutes
Casseroles	High	8 minutes
Beefburgers	High	1 minute each side
Mince	High	5 minutes
Chops	High	6-7 minutes
Bacon rashers	High	4 minutes
Gammon steaks	High	3 minutes
Liver	High	4 minutes
Kidneys (2-3)	High	3-5 minutes
Cod steaks and fillets	High	4 minutes
Plaice fillets	High	3 minutes
Sole fillets	High	3-4 minutes
Mackerel, whole	High	4 minutes each side
Trout, whole	High	4½ minutes each side

COOKING TIMES FOR FRESH VEGETABLES

Type	Water	Setting	Cooking time per 450g (1 lb)
Artichokes, globe	120 ml (4 fl oz)	High	7-8 minutes
Artichokes, Jerusalem, cubed	120 ml (4 fl oz)	High	12-14 minutes
Asparagus	85 ml (3 fl oz)	High	8-10 minutes
Aubergine, diced	2 tbls	High	6 minutes
Beans, green	120 ml (4 fl oz)	High	6-8 minutes
Beans, broad	175 ml (6 fl oz)	High	8 minutes
Beetroot, halved	120 ml (4 fl oz)	High	7-8 minutes
Broccoli	120 ml (4 fl oz)	High	10-12 minutes
Brussels sprouts	50 ml (2 fl oz)	High	7-8 minutes
Cabbage, quartered	120 ml (4 fl oz)	High	10-12 minutes
Cabbage, shredded	120 ml (4 fl oz)	High	9-11 minutes
Carrots, whole (6 medium)	120 ml (4 fl oz)	High	10-12 minutes
Carrots, sliced	120 ml (4 fl oz)	High	10-12 minutes
Cauliflower, whole	120 ml (4 fl oz)	High	10-12 minutes
Cauliflower, florets	120 ml (4 fl oz)	High	8-10 minutes
Celery	50 ml (2 fl oz)	High	14-16 minutes
Chicory, whole (4 medium)	50 ml (2 fl oz)	High	5-8 minutes
Corn on the cob (2)	50 ml (2 fl oz)	High	6-8 minutes
Fennel, quartered	50 ml (2 fl oz)	High	12-14 minutes
Leeks, sliced	50 ml (2 fl oz)	High	10-12 minutes
Marrow, sliced	—	High	8-10 minutes
Mushrooms	2 tbls	High	4-5 minutes
Okra	120 ml (4 fl oz)	High	5 minutes
Onions (4 medium)	50 ml (2 fl oz)	High	10-12 minutes
Parsnips, cubed	120 ml (4 fl oz)	High	12-14 minutes
Peas, shelled	120 ml (4 fl oz)	High	6-8 minutes
Potatoes, baked in skin (2 medium)	—	High	7-9 minutes
Potatoes, (peeled and quartered)	120 ml (4 fl oz)	High	10-14 minutes
Pumpkin, swedes and turnips, cubed	120 ml (4 fl oz)	High	14-16 minutes
Salsify, cubed	120 ml (4 fl oz)	High	12-14 minutes
Spinach	—	High	6-8 minutes
Tomatoes, halved	—	High	1½-2 minutes

COOKING TIMES FOR FROZEN VEGETABLES

Type	Water	Setting	Cooking time on HIGH per 450 g (1 lb)
Artichoke hearts	2 tbls	High	4 minutes
Asparagus tips	4 tbls	High	6-7 minutes
Beans, green	120 ml (4 fl oz)	High	7-9 minutes
Broccoli	120 ml (4 fl oz)	High	7-9 minutes
Brussels sprouts	120 ml (4 fl oz)	High	6-7 minutes
Cabbage, shredded	85 ml (3 fl oz)	High	8-10 minutes
Carrots	50 ml (2 fl oz)	High	5-7 minutes
Cauliflower florets	50 ml (2 fl oz)	High	5-7 minutes
Corn on the cob (2)	—	High	8 minutes
Corn kernels	2 tbls	High	5-7 minutes
Courgettes, sliced	—	High	5-6 minutes
Mushrooms	—	High	5-7 minutes
Onions, small, whole	—	High	4-6 minutes
Peas	50 ml (2 fl oz)	High	5-6 minutes
Peas and carrots mixed	2 tbls	High	6-7 minutes
Peppers, diced (6 oz)	50 ml (2 fl oz)	High	6-7 minutes
Potatoes, new	50 ml (2 fl oz)	High	7-8 minutes
Spinach	—	High	6-7 minutes

DEFROSTING TIMES FOR MEAT, POULTRY

Food	Setting	Defrosting time per 450 g (1 lb)
Beef joints	Low	9 minutes
Beef mince	Low	10 minutes
Beef, large steak	Low	8 minutes
Lamb joints	Low	10 minutes
Lamb chops	Low	5 minutes
Pork	Low	8½ minutes
Veal	Low	9 minutes
Chicken whole	Low	6 minutes
Chicken pieces	Low	5 minutes
Liver	Low	4 minutes
Kidney	Low	4 minutes
Casseroles	Low	15-20 minutes

Carrot and coriander soup

SERVES 4-6

50g (2oz) butter
1 onion, finely chopped
450g (1 lb) carrots, finely chopped
3 tbls sherry
3 tbls orange juice
2 tsp ground coriander seeds
salt and pepper
600 ml (1 pint) stock
142 ml (5 fl oz) carton single cream
chopped coriander leaves

In a 2½-3 litre (5 pint) casserole, melt the butter on **High** for 30 seconds. Stir in the onions and cook for 3 minutes on **High**. Add the carrot, sherry, orange juice, coriander and seasoning. Cover the casserole and microwave on **High** for 6 minutes.

Stir in the stock and cover and microwave on **Medium** for 20 minutes. Allow to cool slightly and then liquidize the soup. Adjust seasoning. Stir in the cream. Return the soup to the casserole and microwave on **High** for about 6 minutes until hot.

To serve, sprinkle with freshly chopped coriander leaves.

● Carrot and coriander soup

French onion soup

SERVES 6

2 large onions, thinly sliced
1 garlic clove, crushed
½ tsp sugar
40 g (1½ oz) butter, diced
2 tbls plain flour
600 ml (1 pint) boiling water
pinch of English mustard powder
1 beef stock cube, crumbled
300 ml (½ pint) canned beef
    consommé
½ tsp Worcestershire sauce
salt and pepper
6 thick slices French bread, toasted
50 g (2 oz) Cheddar or Emmenthal
    cheese, grated

Combine the onions, garlic, sugar and butter in a large bowl and microwave on **High** for 6-8 minutes until the onions are soft. Stir several times during cooking.

Mix the flour with a little of the water to a smooth paste. Add more water until the flour liquid is thin but smooth. Stir in the flour mixture, the rest of the water, mustard, stock cube, consommé and Worcestershire sauce. Partially cover with cling film and microwave on **High** for 20 minutes, stirring several times during cooking. Leave to stand for 5 minutes, then season.

Sprinkle the toasted bread with cheese and brown under a pre-heated grill. Serve immediately in heated individual soup bowls, each one topped with a slice of cheese toast.

Country vegetable soup

SERVES 4

25 g (1 oz) margarine or butter
100 g (4 oz) cabbage, finely shredded
1 potato, diced
1 onion, chopped
2 carrots, thinly sliced
½ red pepper, cored, seeded and
    diced
50 g (2 oz) turnip, diced
397 g (14 oz) can tomatoes
salt and pepper
900 ml (1½ pints) hot beef stock

Place all the ingredients except the stock in a large bowl. Cover with cling film and microwave on **High** for 10 minutes, stirring halfway through.

Stir in the stock. Cover and microwave on **High** for 10 minutes or until the vegetables are tender, stirring halfway through cooking.

Adjust seasoning to taste before serving in heated individual soup bowls.

Serving idea: Serve with chunks of wholemeal bread and butter for a warming winter's night supper.

Variations: Vary the vegetables according to availability: try Brussels sprouts, swede, parsnip or celery.

Chicken and spinach soup

SERVES 4

1.2 litres (2 pints) chicken stock
1 chicken breast, skinned
100 g (4 oz) spinach, stalks removed
  and shredded
2 tbls grated Parmesan cheese
salt and pepper
1 egg, beaten

Pour the stock into a large bowl, add the chicken breast, then cover with pierced cling film and microwave on **High** for 10-12 minutes.

Using a slotted spoon, remove the chicken, discard the bone and shred the flesh finely.

Add the shredded chicken and spinach to the stock and, without covering, microwave on **High** for 5 minutes.

Stir in the cheese and season to taste. Microwave on **High** for 2 minutes or until boiling.

Pour the soup into a heated serving tureen and quickly strain the beaten egg over the soup. Serve at once.

Serving idea: Serve with warm crusty rolls.
Variation: For a more distinctive flavour, use sorrel instead of spinach.

● Chicken and spinach soup; French onion soup; Country vegetable soup

15

Corn and crab soup

SERVES 4-6

1 small onion, finely chopped
1 celery stalk, finely chopped
1 back bacon rasher, chopped
25 g (1 oz) butter, diced
25 g (1 oz) plain flour
600 ml (1 pint) milk
300 ml (½ pint) water
1 bay leaf
198 g (7 oz) can creamed sweetcorn
198 g (7 oz) crabmeat, flaked
salt and pepper

Combine the onion, celery, bacon and butter in a large bowl. Microwave on **High** for 4 minutes, stirring once during cooking.

Stir in the flour and microwave on **High** for 2 minutes. Add the milk, water and bay leaf and microwave for a further 6 minutes, stirring every 2 minutes. Pour into another bowl.

Add the sweetcorn to the sauce with the crab.

Microwave on **High** for 4 minutes until hot. Season to taste and serve in heated individual soup bowls.

Serving idea: Serve with toast and butter.
Variations: Either fresh, frozen or drained canned crabmeat can be successfully used in this soup.

Smoked haddock starter

• Left: Smoked haddock starter
Right: Corn and crab soup

SERVES 4

100 g (4 oz) mushrooms, finely sliced
1 small onion, finely chopped
25 g (1 oz) margarine or butter, diced
25 g (1 oz) plain flour
250 ml (8 fl oz) milk
175 g (6 oz) cooked smoked haddock,
*   skinned and flaked*
salt and pepper
350 g (12 oz) cooked mashed potato

Combine the mushrooms, onion and margarine in a bowl and microwave on **High** for 4 minutes.

Stir in the flour, then gradually stir in the milk. Stir in the haddock and season to taste.

Microwave on **High** for 4 minutes. Stir several times during cooking.

Pipe the mashed potato around the edges of 4 individual gratin dishes.

Spoon the haddock mixture into the centre of each dish and place under a preheated grill for 1-2 minutes to brown the potato.

Serving idea: Serve with lemon twists and thin brown bread and butter.

17

Hot avocado with prawns

SERVES 4

15 g (½ oz) butter
2 tbls plain flour
150 ml (¼ pint) milk
salt
¼ tsp cayenne pepper
225 g (8 oz) peeled prawns
2 avocados
2 tbls lemon juice
To finish
50 g (2 oz) Gruyère cheese, grated
cayenne pepper

Place the butter in a bowl. Microwave on **High** for 30 seconds, until melted.

Stir in the flour, then microwave on **High** for 30 seconds. Gradually stir in the milk. Season, then stir in the prawns.

Microwave on **High** for 5½ minutes, stirring several times during cooking.

Halve the avocados and remove the stones. Sprinkle with the lemon juice. Arrange the avocado halves in a flameproof dish. Divide the prawn mixture equally among them, making sure it covers the flesh completely. Sprinkle with the Gruyère cheese and a little cayenne.

Place under a preheated grill until the cheese has melted.

Mushrooms in tomato sauce

SERVES 4

6 tbls olive oil
1 onion, finely chopped
450 g (1 lb) tomatoes, skinned, seeded and chopped
2 garlic cloves, crushed
1 tsp dried oregano
salt and pepper
275 g (10 oz) button mushrooms

Place half the oil and the onion in a bowl. Microwave on **High** for 3 minutes, stirring several times during cooking.

Add the tomatoes, garlic and oregano and season to taste. Without covering, microwave on **High** for 5 minutes, stirring halfway through cooking.

Add the mushrooms and microwave on **High** for 5 minutes or until tender.

Spoon the mixture into a serving bowl and stir in the remaining oil. Allow to cool, then chill in the refrigerator for 3-4 hours before serving.

Serving idea: Serve with hot herb bread.

Coquilles St Jacques

SERVES 4

275 g (10 oz) fresh or frozen scallops
150 ml (5 fl oz) dry, white wine
¼ tsp dried savory
1 bay leaf
salt and pepper
225 g (8 oz) mushrooms, sliced
25 g (1 oz) butter
15 g (½ oz) flour
1 tbls lemon juice
120 ml (4 fl oz) single cream
15 g (½ oz) fresh breadcrumbs toasted
paprika

Defrost the scallops if frozen. Cut into quarters and set aside.

Combine the wine, savory, bay leaf, salt and pepper in a 900 ml (1½ pint) heat-resistant dish. Add the scallops and mushrooms. Cook on **High** for 3 minutes. Drain, reserving 150 ml (¼ pint) of the stock. Put all the butter into a 600 ml (1 pint) heat-resistant dish. Cook for 20 seconds until melted. Blend in the flour to form a smooth paste. Gradually stir in the stock, lemon juice and then the cream. Cook on **High** for 2-3 minutes until the sauce thickens. Stir every 30 seconds. Mix the scallops and mushrooms with the sauce and cook on **High** for 6 minutes until the mixture is heated.

Spoon into scallop shells or ramekins. Garnish with breadcrumbs and paprika just before serving.

18

● Coquilles St Jacques; Mushrooms in tomato sauce; Hot avocado with prawns

Country-style pâté

SERVES 4

4 streaky bacon rashers, rinds
    removed
50 g (2 oz) butter, diced
225 g (8 oz) pig's liver
225 g (8 oz) chicken livers
75 g (3 oz) fresh white breadcrumbs
1 egg, beaten
1 garlic clove, crushed
3 tbls red wine
1 tbls brandy
1 tsp chopped fresh thyme or
    ½ tsp dried thyme
25 g (1 oz) blanched almonds,
    coarsely chopped
salt and pepper

Lay the bacon rashers flat on a board and stretch with the back of a knife. Use to line a 450 g (1 lb) microware loaf tin.

Combine the butter, pig's and chicken livers in a bowl. Cover and microwave on **High** for about 10 minutes, stirring several times during cooking, or until the livers are cooked.

Process in a blender or food processor until smooth. Add all the remaining ingredients and process for a further 30 seconds until well combined.

Spoon the mixture into the prepared tin and fold over the ends of the bacon.

Cover with cling film and microwave on **High** for 5 minutes.

Cover the tin with foil, weight down and chill in the refrigerator overnight. Turn out on to a serving plate and slice.

Eggs benedict

SERVES 4

250 ml (8 fl oz) water
4 tbls white wine vinegar
4 eggs
4 slices lean cooked ham
2 toasted muffins, halved and
*   buttered*
hollandaise sauce (see page 60)
watercress sprigs, to garnish

Divide the water and vinegar equally among 4 ramekin dishes. Without covering, microwave on **High** for 2 minutes or until boiling. Using oven gloves to handle the dishes, break an egg into each one.

● Left: Country-style pâté
Right: Eggs benedict

Microwave on **High** for 2 minutes. Leave to stand for 1 minute, then pour off the liquid.

Meanwhile trim the ham to fit the muffins. Place a piece of ham on each half muffin and keep warm.

Place the poached eggs on the ham and muffins and spoon over the hollandaise sauce. Garnish with watercress sprigs and serve immediately.

Variations: Toasted baps or crumpets may be used instead of muffins.

21

Ratatouille

SERVES 4

*2 aubergines, cut into 1 cm (½ inch)
  cubes*
salt
2 tbls vegetable oil
2 onions, sliced
*2 green peppers, cored, seeded and
  sliced*
450 g (1 lb) courgettes, sliced
397 g (14 oz) can tomatoes with juice
pepper

Place the aubergines in a colander set over a plate and sprinkle with salt. Leave for 30 minutes to drain, then rinse under cold running water and pat dry with absorbent kitchen paper.

Place the oil in a casserole and microwave on **High** for 45 seconds.

Add the onions and microwave on **High** for 5 minutes.

Add the aubergines, peppers, and courgettes and stir. Cover with cling film and microwave on **High** for 8 minutes.

Add the tomatoes with their juice and season to taste with salt and pepper. Cover and microwave on **High** for 5 minutes.

Stir, then microwave on **Low** for a further 8 minutes.

Serving ideas: Serve with plainly grilled steak or lamb or pork chops, or with pasta or brown rice for a vegetarian meal.
Variation: Ripe fresh tomatoes, skinned and chopped, may replace the canned tomatoes.

● Ratatouille; Courgettes with nutmeg
Glazed mange-tout

Glazed mange-tout

SERVES 4

6 tbls water
½ tsp salt
*350 g (12 oz) mange-tout, topped and
  tailed*
15 g (½ oz) butter, diced
mint sprigs, to garnish

Combine the water and salt in a large shallow dish. Add the mange-tout, cover with cling film and microwave on **High** for 6-7 minutes, stirring several

times during cooking.

Leave to stand, covered, for 5 minutes. Drain, add the butter and mint and toss well. Serve hot.

Serving idea: Serve with roast lamb.

Courgettes with nutmeg

SERVES 4

12 medium courgettes, trimmed and halved
40 g (1½ oz) unsalted butter
½-1 tsp grated nutmeg
salt and pepper

Score each courgette lengthways with the prongs of a fork.

Place the butter and nutmeg in a shallow dish and microwave on **High** for 30 seconds. Arrange the courgettes in a single layer in the dish and microwave on **High** for 3 minutes.

Rearrange the courgettes, transferring those in the centre to the edge of the dish. Baste with butter, cover loosely with cling film and microwave on **High** for 4 minutes, giving the dish a half-turn after 2 minutes.

Leave to stand, covered, for 5 minutes. If any of the courgettes still feel hard, microwave these on **High** for a further 30 seconds.

Transfer the courgettes to a heated serving dish, season well with salt and pepper and pour over the cooking butter. Serve hot.

Serving idea: Serve with pork chops, grilled steaks or fish. These courgettes are also good with Italian dishes.

23

Vegetable curry

SERVES 4

1 tbls oil
1 small green pepper, deseeded and
  chopped
1 onion, finely sliced
1 clove garlic, crushed
3 large tomatoes
225 g (8 oz) cauliflower, cut into tiny
  sprigs
225 g (8 oz) aubergines, diced
25 g (1 oz) brown sugar
1 tbls lemon juice
1 tsp ground turmeric
1-2 tbls garam masala (curry spices)
2 tbls plain flour
300 ml (½ pint) hot stock
1 tbls sultanas
salt and pepper

Put the oil, green pepper, onion and garlic, into a large casserole. Cover and microwave on **High** for 5 minutes.

To skin the tomatoes place on a plate and microwave on **High** for 30 seconds to 1 minute until the skin can be peeled off easily. Skin and chop, then stir into the casserole with the cauliflower, aubergines, brown sugar, lemon juice, turmeric, and garam masala. Cover and microwave on **High** for 10 minutes stirring halfway through cooking.

Stir in the flour, hot stock, sultanas and seasoning. Cover and cook for 4 minutes on **High**.

Serving idea: Serve with boiled rice and a lentil dish accompanied by poppadums.

• Left: Vegetable curry
Above: Broccoli in ham and cheese sauce

Broccoli in ham and cheese sauce

SERVES 4

450 g (1 lb) frozen broccoli spears
2 tbls water
25 g (1 oz) butter
25 g (1 oz) plain flour
300 ml (½ pint) milk
50 g (2 oz) ham, finely chopped
75 g (3 oz) cheddar cheese, grated
1 tsp wholegrain mustard
salt and pepper

Defrost and cook broccoli with the water on **High** for about 7-8 minutes. Drain. Arrange in a 1.2 litre (2 pint) dish.

Melt the butter in a glass 1.75 litre (3 pint) bowl for 30 seconds on **High**. Add the flour and microwave on **High** for 30 seconds.

Gradually stir in the milk. Microwave on **High** for 3-4 minutes until the sauce is thick. Whisk well.

Stir in the ham, 50 g (2 oz) of the cheese, mustard and seasoning. Pour over the broccoli and sprinkle with the remaining cheese. Microwave on **High** for 7 minutes.

Serving ideas: Serve with brown rice or with Stuffed jacket potatoes (see page 26) and a salad.

Stuffed peppers

SERVES 4

4 peppers (2 red and 2 yellow)
397 g (14 oz) can tomatoes, drained
  and chopped
100 g (4 oz) long-grain rice, cooked
1 garlic clove, crushed
salt and pepper
1 tbls chopped fresh rosemary or
  1 tsp dried rosemary
175 g (6 oz) mozzarella cheese, cubed
6 anchovy fillets, chopped
2 tbls grated Parmesan cheese
2 tbls olive oil
150 ml (¼ pint) water

Cut a thin slice from the stalk end of each pepper. Carefully remove the seeds and pith, making sure you do not pierce the pepper shells.

Combine all the remaining ingredients, except the oil and water, and spoon into the pepper shells.

Stand the stuffed peppers upright in a shallow dish into which they fit closely together. Spoon over the oil.

Pour the water into the dish and cover loosely with cling film. Microwave on **High** for 10-12 minutes or until the peppers are tender.

Leave to stand covered for 2 minutes, then drain off the water. Serve hot.

Serving ideas: Serve for lunch or supper with salad and hot French bread.

Bacon and egg stuffed tomatoes

SERVES 4

4 large beefsteak tomatoes
4 eggs
4 lean bacon rashers, rinded

Cut a slice from the top of each tomato and set aside.

Using a teaspoon, scoop out half the pulp from the tomatoes. Arrange the tomato shells side by side on a serving plate and break an egg into each one.

Wrap a rasher of bacon around each tomato and secure with a cocktail stick. Spoon the reserved pulp over the eggs and top with the tomato lids.

Cover with absorbent kitchen paper and microwave on **High** for about 4-6 minutes, or until the egg white just begins to set.

Leave to stand for 1 minute, remove the paper and serve hot.

Serving ideas: Serve for high tea, with hot buttered toast, or as part of a brunch menu.

Stuffed jacket potatoes

4 medium potatoes
  washed and dried
75 g (3 oz) Gruyère or Double
  Gloucester cheese, grated
1 tbls tomato ketchup
1 tbls Worcestershire sauce
15 g (½ oz) butter, or 1 tbls soured
  cream
salt and pepper
chopped fresh chives or parsley, to
  garnish

Place the potatoes on a tray or paper towel, prick them and cook for 6 minutes on **High**. Turn the potatoes over and cook for a further 7 minutes.

Wrap each potato in foil and leave to stand for 5 minutes. Cut each potato in half lengthways. Scoop out the flesh, leaving the potato shell intact. Mix the potato flesh with the cheese, tomato ketchup, Worcestershire sauce, butter, salt and pepper. Pile the mixture back into the potato jackets and microwave on **High** for 3-4 minutes. Serve garnished with chives or parsley.

Variation: use cream or curd cheese instead of the grated cheese and replace the Worcestershire sauce with chilli sauce.

● **Stuffed jacket potatoes; Bacon and egg stuffed tomatoes; Stuffed peppers**

Spicy pilaff

SERVES 4

50 g (2 oz) butter
225 g (8 oz) long-grain rice
50 g (2 oz) hazelnuts, finely chopped
600 ml (1 pint) hot chicken or beef
*   stock*
½ tsp salt
1 tsp ground cardamom
½ tsp turmeric
25 g (1 oz) sultanas

Put the butter in a large deep casserole and microwave on **High** for 1 minute. Stir in the rice. Microwave on **High** for 3 minutes, stirring halfway through cooking.

● Centre: Risotto with spinach and herbs
Right: Spicy pilaff

Add the hazelnuts and microwave on **High** for 2 minutes.

Stir in the stock, salt, cardamom, turmeric and sultanas. Microwave on **High** for 12-15 minutes, stirring half-way through cooking.

Stir, then cover tightly and leave to stand for 5 minutes before serving.

Serving ideas: Serve as an accompaniment to your favourite curry dish, along with a salad of sliced tomatoes and onion rings, sprinkled with chopped fresh herbs.

28

Risotto with spinach and herbs

SERVES 4-6

2 tbls olive oil
100 g (4 oz) butter
1 onion, finely chopped
100 g (4 oz) mushrooms, sliced
450 g (1 lb) Italian risotto rice (try Arborio)
1.6 litres (2¾ pints) hot chicken stock
225 g (8 oz) cooked spinach, chopped
1 tsp dried oregano
1 garlic clove, crushed
salt and pepper
75 g (3 oz) grated Parmesan or Pecorino cheese
lemon wedges, to garnish

Place the oil and half the butter in a large deep casserole and microwave on **High** for 1 minute. Add the onion and mushrooms and microwave on **High** for 3 minutes.

Stir in the rice. Microwave on **High** for 5 minutes, stirring halfway through cooking.

Add the stock, spinach, oregano, garlic and salt and pepper. Microwave on **High** for 20-25 minutes, stirring several times during cooking, or until the rice is tender and has absorbed all the liquid.

Stir in the remaining butter and the grated cheese. Serve garnished with lemon wedges.

Serving idea: Serve for a TV supper.

Carbonnade of beef

SERVES 4

Note: Most casseroles and stews improve with re-heating in the microwave. If you like your meat very soft, allow the carbonnade to 'rest' for 5-10 minutes in the middle of cooking.

1 tbls oil
2 onions, sliced
4 carrots, sliced
2 streaky bacon rashers, rinded and finely chopped
100 g (4 oz) mushrooms, chopped
700 g (1½ lb) skirt of beef
25 g (1 oz) seasoned flour
300 ml (½ pint) brown ale
150 ml (¼ pint) hot beef stock
2 tsp French mustard
1 tbls freshly chopped parsley
salt and pepper
To finish
8 slices French bread
butter
French mustard

Put the oil, onions, carrots, bacon and mushrooms into a large casserole. Cover and microwave on **High** for 2 minutes.

Cut the meat into 1.5 cm (½ inch) pieces. Toss in the seasoned flour. Add the meat to the vegetables. Pour in the brown ale and stock and add the mustard, parsley and season with salt and plenty of pepper. Microwave on **High** for 5 minutes.

Cover and microwave on **Medium** for 40 minutes. Leave to stand, covered for 10 minutes.

Meanwhile, spread the slices of French bread with butter and mustard. Arrange on top of the casserole and place under a hot grill to crisp the bread.

Chilli con carne

SERVES 4

Note: Use best-quality mince or ground beef for this very popular 'Tex-Mex' dish.

450 g (1 lb) minced beef
1 medium sized onion, chopped
1 clove garlic, crushed
397 g (14 oz) can chopped tomatoes
2 tbls tomato purée
2 tsp chilli powder
salt and pepper
2 tsp Worcestershire sauce
439 g (15½ oz) can red kidney beans, drained
freshly chopped parsley

Place the mince, onion and garlic in a large casserole. Cover and cook on **High** for 5 minutes. Stir meat to break up any lumps.

Add chopped tomatoes, tomato purée, chilli powder, seasoning and Worcestershire sauce. Cover and cook on **High** for 15 minutes. Stir once during cooking.

Add the drained kidney beans, cover and heat on **High** for 3 minutes.

Leave to stand for 5 minutes. Serve sprinkled with chopped parsley.

Serving ideas: Serve accompanied by plain boiled rice and a green salad. Or serve with pitta bread and a salad of finely sliced Spanish onion, sweet peppers and tomatoes dressed in a sharp vinaigrette made with lemon juice.

Chilli con carne also makes an excellent filling for Mexican-style *tacos*.

● **Carbonnade of beef**
Chilli con carne

30

Braised beef

SERVES 4

2 carrots
1 small turnip
1 onion
1 parsnip
25 g (1 oz) butter
1 leek, sliced
1 garlic clove, crushed
700 g (1½ lb) skirt of beef, cut into
   2.5 cm (1 inch) cubes
600 ml (1 pint) beef stock
150 ml (¼ pint) red wine
2 tsp Worcestershire sauce
1 bouquet garni
salt and pepper
25 g (1 oz) cornflour mixed with 3 tbls
   water

Cut the carrots, turnip, onion and parsnip into 1 cm (½ inch) dice.

Place the butter in a large casserole. Microwave on **High** for 1 minute. Stir in the diced vegetables, leek and garlic.

Cover and microwave on **High** for 6 minutes or until the vegetables are tender.

Add the beef, cover and microwave on **High** for 5 minutes, stirring halfway through cooking.

Pour in the stock and wine and add the Worcestershire sauce, bouquet garni and salt and pepper to taste. Cover and microwave on **Medium** for 40 minutes, stirring occasionally. Five minutes before the end of the cooking time stir in the cornflour. Leave to stand, covered, for 10 minutes. Remove the bouquet garni before serving.

Meat loaf

SERVES 4-6

75 g (3 oz) breadcrumbs
1 clove garlic crushed
1 small onion, finely chopped
450 g (1 lb) lean minced beef
2 tbls tomato purée
4 tbls evaporated milk
1 egg, beaten
salt and pepper

In a large bowl mix together all the ingredients thoroughly. Spread the mixture in a 554 g (19½oz) microware loaf pan. Microwave on **High** for 12-15 minutes. Leave to stand for 5 minutes, then turn out on to a serving plate. Serve hot or cold.

● Left: Braised beef
Right: Meat loaf

Serving ideas: Serve hot with a fresh tomato sauce. To serve cold, drain off the juices, leave to cool, then cover and chill in the refrigerator. If liked, the meat loaf may be garnished with cucumber or tomato slices. Slices of the meat loaf, wrapped in foil or cling film, make an excellent addition to a lunch box or picnic basket.
Variations: Substitute pork mince for half the beef and season the mixture with Worcestershire sauce instead of tomato purée.

Chicken marengo

SERVES 4

4 chicken breasts, boned and skinned
2 tbls plain flour
8 spring onions, chopped
25 g (1 oz) butter, softened
100 g (4 oz) mushrooms, sliced
397 g (14 oz) can tomatoes
1 tbls chopped fresh basil or
   1 tsp dried basil
1 tsp chopped fresh thyme or
   ½ tsp dried thyme
2 bay leaves
salt and pepper
1 lemon slice, optional
150 ml (¼ pint) dry white wine
4 cooked peeled king prawns, to
   garnish

Dip the chicken breasts in the flour, to coat thoroughly. Mash the spring onions and butter together.

Preheat a large microware browning skillet for 5 minutes on **High**. Add the spring onion mixture and microwave on **High** for 2 minutes.

Add the chicken and microwave on **High** for 2 minutes. Turn over and microwave on **High** for a further 2 minutes.

Transfer to a casserole. Stir in all the remaining ingredients including any leftover flour, cover with cling film and microwave on **Low** for 20 minutes. Remove the lemon and bay leaves. Serve garnished with the prawns.

Serving ideas: To cook the king prawns for the garnish, place in a dish and cover with water and add a slice of lemon, 1 bay leaf and salt. Cover and microwave on **High** until boiling. Leave to stand for 5 minutes before serving. Plain boiled rice makes the ideal accompaniment.

Variations: Use red wine, Marsala or Madeira in place of the white wine. Veal escalopes may be substituted for the chicken breasts.

Pork vindaloo

SERVES 4

120 ml (4 fl oz) white wine vinegar
450 g (1 lb) pork fillet, cut into 2.5 cm
   (1 inch) cubes
1 large onion, chopped
1 tsp cumin seeds
2 tsp mustard seeds
5 garlic cloves, crushed
½ tsp ground ginger
½ tsp ground cloves
1 tsp ground cinnamon
½ tsp ground black pepper
3 tbls vegetable oil
2 bay leaves
397 g (14 oz) can tomatoes, chopped
½ tsp ground turmeric
salt
chopped fresh coriander, to garnish

Blend 1 tbls of the vinegar with 1 tbls water and toss the pork in this mixture. Drain, pat dry with absorbent kitchen paper, and place in a shallow dish.

Place the onion, cumin seeds, mustard seeds, garlic, ginger, cloves, cinnamon and black pepper in a food processor. Process until smooth, adding enough vinegar to make a thick paste.

Add the spice paste to the pork, mix thoroughly and leave to marinate for 30 minutes.

Place the oil and bay leaves in a large casserole and microwave on **High** for 2 minutes or until golden brown. Add the pork, tomatoes and turmeric, and microwave on **High** for 5 minutes. Add any remaining vinegar and salt to taste.

Cover with cling film and microwave on **Low** for 20 minutes or until the pork is tender. Serve garnished with coriander.

Serving ideas: Serve this hot curry dish with boiled rice and a refreshing cucumber *raita*, accompanied by mango chutney.

• Top: Chicken marengo; Bottom: Pork vindaloo

34

Greek pork kebabs

SERVES 4

450 g (1 lb) pork fillet, cut into 2.5 cm
  (1 inch) cubes
½ green pepper, cored, seeded and
  cut into 8 pieces
½ red pepper, cored, seeded and cut
  into 8 pieces
2 tomatoes, halved
For the marinade
3 tbls olive oil
150 ml (¼ pint) water
175 ml (6 fl oz) chicken stock
2 tbls Worcestershire sauce
1 small onion, sliced
1 tsp mixed dried herbs
1 tbls redcurrant jelly
salt and pepper
For the sauce
25 g (1 oz) butter
25 g (1 oz) plain flour
150 ml (¼ pint) hot chicken stock
2 tbls tomato purée

Combine all the marinade ingredients in a shallow dish. Add the pork cubes, stir well to mix and leave to marinate for 2 hours.

Place the green and red peppers in a bowl, cover with clingfilm and microwave on **High** for 2 minutes.

Drain the pork and reserve the marinade. Thread the pork and peppers alternately on to 4 oiled wooden kebabs skewers. Place on a plate, cover with absorbent kitchen paper and microwave on **High** for 3 minutes.

Place a tomato half on each skewer, cover and microwave on **High** for 4 minutes. Set aside.

To make the sauce, put the butter in a bowl and microwave on **High** for 1 minute. Stir in the flour and microwave on **High** for 30 seconds.

Stir in the strained reserved marinade, hot stock and tomato purée. Microwave on **High** for 3 minutes, stirring every minute.

Serve the kebabs with the sauce.

Serving idea: Serve the kebabs with Spicy pilaff (see page 28).

Dry spiced lamb chops

SERVES 4

4 chump or loin lamb chops
½ tsp chilli powder
2 tsp ground ginger
2 tsp garlic powder
150 g (5.29 oz) carton natural yoghurt
salt and pepper
1 tbls vegetable oil
1 onion, chopped
To garnish
1 lime, cut into wedges
1 small onion, cut into rings

Place the chops in a shallow dish. Mix the chilli, ginger and garlic powder with the yoghurt and season to taste with salt and pepper. Pour the mixture over the chops and leave to marinate for 2 hours.

Place the oil and onion in a shallow dish and microwave on **High** for 3 minutes.

Arrange the chops in the dish, thin ends towards the middle, pour over the marinade, cover and microwave on **Low** for about 30 minutes, or until tender, turning the chops over halfway through cooking. Brown under a grill to finish, if liked, and serve garnished with lime wedges and onion rings.

Serving ideas: Serve the chops with a mixed salad well dressed with oil and vinegar and jacket-baked potatoes with sour cream and chives, or a potato salad with a mayonnaise-based dressing.

Variations: Pork chops may be successfully substituted for lamb. Lemon wedges and spring onion tassels, or tomato slices and watercress sprigs make attractive alternatives for the garnish.

● Top: Greek pork kebabs
Bottom: Dry spiced lamb chops

Chinese chicken

SERVES 4

8 chicken drumsticks, skinned
8 spring onions, finely chopped
½ green pepper, cored, seeded and
*   diced*
½ red pepper, cored, seeded and
*   diced*
2 garlic cloves, crushed
25 g (1 oz) butter, diced
1 tbls cornflour
¼ tsp five spice powder
about 300 ml (½ pint) hot chicken
*   stock*
2 tbls red wine vinegar
1 tbls dark soy sauce
grated rind of 1 orange
50 g (2 oz) soft light brown sugar

Place the chicken in a bowl, cover with pierced cling film and microwave on **High** for 13-15 minutes, rearranging halfway through cooking. Set aside, covered.

Place the spring onions, peppers and garlic in a bowl, cover and microwave on **High** for 5 minutes, stirring halfway through cooking. Stir in the butter, cover and microwave on **High** for 2 minutes.

Stir in the cornflour and five spice powder. Make the chicken juices up to 300 ml (½ pint) with the stock, then stir in the remaining ingredients.

Cover and microwave on **High** for 3 minutes, stirring halfway through cooking.

Add the chicken, cover and microwave on **High** for 3-4 minutes.

Bacon with pineapple

SERVES 6-8

1-1.5 kg (2-3 lb) rinded bacon joint
cloves
2 × 439 g (15½ oz) cans pineapple
rings, drained with syrup reserved
2 tbls soft light brown sugar
1 tsp French mustard
¼ tsp ground ginger
maraschino cherries

Score the fat surface of the bacon diagonally, to make a trellis pattern, and stud with cloves.

Place the bacon in a roasting bag. Combine the pineapple syrup, sugar, mustard and ginger and pour into the bag. Leave to marinate for 1 hour.

Place the bacon in the bag in a dish and loosely fold over the top of the bag.

Microwave on **Medium** for 20-30 minutes, or until tender. Place the bacon on a heated serving plate, pour over the juices and serve surrounded by the pineapple rings and cherries.

Serving ideas: Serve with jacket-baked potatoes and sliced green beans, or Broccoli in ham and cheese sauce (see page 25).

Variations: Canned peach or apricot halves may be used instead of pineapple.

● **Left: Chinese chicken**
Right: Bacon with pineapple

Potato and salami omelette

• Centre: Potato and salami omelette
Right: Seafood risotto

SERVES 4

2 medium potatoes, grated
175 g (6 oz) salami. chopped
6 eggs, lightly beaten
salt and pepper
1 garlic clove, crushed
1 tbls chopped fresh parsley
25 g (1 oz) grated Parmesan or
   Pecorino cheese
40 g (1 ½ oz) butter

Drain the potatoes on absorbent kitchen paper. Place the potatoes and salami in a bowl, cover with cling film and microwave on **High** for 5 minutes, stirring once during cooking. Set aside.

Add all the remaining ingredients, except the butter, to the beaten eggs.

Place the butter in a round shallow 20-23 cm (8-9 inch) microware dish. Microwave on **High** for 30 seconds. Tilt the dish to coat the bottom evenly with the butter.

Pour in the egg mixture and microwave on **High** for 3 minutes, stirring twice during cooking.

Drain off any fat and stir in the potato and salami mixture until thoroughly mixed.

Microwave on **High** for 2 minutes or until the omelette is set. Brown under a grill if liked.

Serving ideas: Serve with French fries and a mixed salad.

40

Seafood risotto

SERVES 4

50 g (2 oz) butter
1 large onion, finely chopped
½ green pepper, cored, seeded and
  finely diced
½ red pepper, cored, seeded and
  finely diced
2 tbls tomato purée
1 garlic clove, crushed
1 tsp mixed dried herbs
50 g (2 oz) mushrooms, finely chopped
350 g (12 oz) long-grain rice
750 ml (1¼ pints) hot chicken stock
¼ tsp vegetable oil
salt and pepper
225 g (8 oz) white fish fillets
225 g (8 oz) peeled prawns
225 g (8 oz) crabmeat, flaked

Place the butter, onion, green and red peppers, tomato purée, garlic, herbs and mushrooms in a large bowl. Cover with cling film and microwave on **High** for 7-8 minutes, stirring halfway through cooking.

Stir in the rice, stock, oil and salt and pepper to taste. Cover and microwave on **High** for 13 minutes, stirring halfway through cooking. Set aside, covered.

Place the white fish in a shallow dish. Cover and microwave on **High** for 2 minutes. Leave to stand for 2 minutes, then remove any skin and bones and flake the flesh. Set aside while cooking the prawns and crabmeat.

Place the prawns and crabmeat in a bowl and microwave on **High** for 5 minutes.

Stir the white fish, prawns and crabmeat into the rice mixture and microwave on **High** for 1 minute to reheat.

41

• Above: Mustard herrings; Right: Sole in tomato and mushroom sauce

Mustard herrings

SERVES 2

15 g (½ oz) butter
1 tbls lemon juice
salt
1 tbls coarse-grained mustard
2 × 450 g (1 lb) herrings, cleaned and
   gutted
1 tbls plain flour

Place the butter in a shallow dish. Microwave on **High** for 30 seconds. Stir in the lemon juice, salt and mustard.

Coat the herrings in the flour, put them in the dish and turn to coat with the butter mixture.

Arrange the herrings head to tail, cover with kitchen paper and microwave on **High** for 3-4 minutes or until tender. Turn the herrings over halfway through cooking.

Serving ideas: Serve garnished with lemon twists, accompanied by wholemeal bread and butter or a rice salad for a light supper dish.

Sole in tomato and mushroom sauce

SERVES 4

1 small bunch spring onions, thinly
   sliced
25 g (1 oz) butter
225 g (8 oz) mushrooms, sliced
450 g (1 lb) tomatoes, skinned and
   quartered
2 tbls chopped fresh parsley
2 tsp basil
pinch of sugar
salt and pepper
4 Dover soles, each about 350 g
   (12 oz), skinned

Place the spring onions and butter in a large shallow dish. Microwave on **High** for 3 minutes. Add the mushrooms and microwave on **High** for 3 minutes.

Stir in the tomatoes, parsley, basil, sugar and salt and pepper to taste and cover loosely with cling film. Microwave on **Low** for 15 minutes. Set aside, covered.

Place each sole on a serving plate. Season to taste and cover with cling film. Microwave individually on **High** for 4 minutes each. Keep warm while microwaving the remainder.

Stir the sauce thoroughly to break up the vegetables. Spoon the sauce over the fish and serve.

Serving ideas: The fish can be cooked all at once by stacking the plates using special microwave stacking equipment. Microwave on **High** for 12 minutes, altering the position of each plate several times during cooking. Serve with new potatoes and French beans.

Chocolate mousse

SERVES 4

150 g (5 oz) plain chocolate
4 tbls cold strong black coffee
25 g (1 oz) butter, softened
3 tbls sugar
1 tsp brandy
75 g (3 oz) blanched almonds, toasted
    and chopped
175 ml (6 fl oz) double cream
grated chocolate, to decorate

Place the chocolate and coffee in a bowl and microwave on **High** for 3 minutes or until the chocolate has melted.

Beat thoroughly, then stir in the butter, sugar, brandy and almonds. Allow to cool slightly.

Whip the cream until it forms soft peaks. Fold most of the cream into the chocolate mixture and reserve the remainder for decoration.

Divide the mixture between 4 ramekin dishes and chill in the refrigerator.

Whip the remaining cream stiffly and pipe over each serving. Sprinkle with grated chocolate.

Christmas pudding

SERVES 6-8

200 g (7 oz) shredded suet
175 g (6 oz) fresh white breadcrumbs
450 g (1 lb) mixed dried fruit
100 g (4 oz) chopped mixed peel
175 g (6 oz) plain flour
50 g (2 oz) ground almonds
225 g (8 oz) soft dark brown sugar
1 tsp ground cinnamon
½ tsp ground mace
½ tsp ground ginger
⅛ tsp salt
3 medium cooking apples, peeled,
  cored and finely chopped
grated rind and juice of 1 orange
grated rind and juice of 1 lemon
2 tbls brandy
6 eggs
2 tbls black treacle

Combine all the dry ingredients in a mixing bowl. Add all the remaining ingredients and stir well to mix.

Spoon the mixture into 2 lightly greased 900 ml (1½ pint) pudding basins. Cover with cling film and microwave, one at a time, on **High** for 10 minutes.

Leave to stand, covered, until cooled. Pour a little extra brandy over the puddings if liked.

Serving ideas: Store covered in the refrigerator until required. Reheat in the microwave on **High** for 5 minutes. Leave to stand for 4 minutes, then microwave on **High** for a further 3 minutes. Serve with brandy butter or whipped cream.

● Left: Chocolate mousse
Right: Christmas pudding

Caramelized oranges

SERVES 4

4 large oranges
25 g (1 oz) unsalted butter
50 g (2 oz) Demerara sugar
1 tbls chopped mint
20 cloves
4 sprigs mint to decorate
For the syrup
100 g (4 oz) caster sugar
4 tbls water
2 tbls hot water

Grate the rind from 2 oranges and set aside. Remove all the pith from the oranges and cut each one crossways into 4 or 5 slices. Blend the butter with half the sugar and the chopped mint.

Spread a little of the mixture over each orange slice, then reassemble the slices to form whole oranges. Spread the remaining mixture on top of the oranges and sprinkle with the remaining sugar and orange rind. Push a wooden cocktail stick through each orange to secure. Press 5 cloves into each orange.

To make the caramel syrup, spread the sugar out in a shallow glass dish, and sprinkle with 4 tbls water. Microwave on **High** for 1 minute. Stir well and microwave on **High** for a further 1 minute. Stir again to make sure the sugar is dissolved. Microwave on **High** for 5-6 minutes. Watch carefully towards the end and remove the caramel when it is just beginning to turn golden brown as it will continue to cook in the dish.

Cool for a minute then carefully add the hot water. The mixture will spit and bubble slightly at first. Stir well to make a caramel sauce.

Place the oranges in the syrup and microwave on **High** for 1 minute. Baste with the syrup and microwave on **High** for a further minute. Baste well. Allow to cool, basting from time to time with the sauce. Serve decorated with mint.

Strawberry soufflé

SERVES 8

2 tbls medium white wine
4 tbls water
15 g (½ oz) sachet powdered gelatine
450 g (1 lb) strawberries, puréed
1½ tbls lemon juice
100 g (4 oz) caster sugar
284 ml (10 fl oz) carton double cream,
    stiffly whipped
6 egg whites, stiffly whisked
For the decoration
284 ml (10 fl oz) carton double cream,
    stiffly whipped (optional)
strawberries

Place the wine, water and gelatine in a basin and stir well. Microwave on **High** for 30 seconds, stirring to dissolve the gelatine.

Add the strawberry purée, lemon juice and sugar and stir well. Leave to cool, stirring several times.

Fold the cream into the strawberry mixture, then gently fold in the egg whites, using a large metal spoon.

Tie strips of lightly oiled greaseproof paper around the outside of 8 individual ramekin dishes, oiled side inwards, to come 1 cm (½ inch) above the rims. Spoon the soufflé mixture into the ramekins and chill in the refrigerator for 2-3 hours or until set.

Remove paper. Decorate with cream, if liked, and sliced strawberries.

Serving ideas: Serve with dainty crisp biscuits. This soufflé makes a perfect dinner party finale. A dessert wine such as Sauternes or any sweet white or rosé wine would make an ideal accompaniment.

Variations: Raspberries, blackberries or a mixture of soft fruits may be used instead of the strawberries. Cointreau may replace the white wine.

● Top: Strawberry soufflé; Bottom: Caramelized oranges

Lime meringue pie

SERVES 4

shortcrust pastry made from
100 g (4 oz) flour
finely grated rind of 2 limes
120 ml (4 fl oz) fresh lime juice
  (approx. 4 limes)
25 g (1 oz) cornflour
200 g (7 oz) caster sugar
2 egg yolks, beaten
2 egg whites

Roll out the pastry and use to line a 15 cm (6 inch) microware pie dish. Prick the pastry all over with a fork and microwave on **High** for 5 minutes.

Make up the lime rind and juice with cold water to 300 ml (½ pint).

In a large jug mix the cornflour with a little of the lime water to make a smooth paste. Gradually stir in the remaining lime water. Microwave on **High** for 3½ minutes or until the mixture thickens. Stir once every minute.

Whisk 75 g (3 oz) of the sugar with the egg yolks. Beat into the lime mixture. Pour into the prepared pastry case and leave to cool.

Whisk the egg whites until stiff. Fold in the remaining sugar, pile over the filling and swirl attractively. Microwave on **High** for 1½ minutes. Place under a hot grill for a few seconds to brown the meringue, if liked. Serve hot or cold.

Variation: For a lemon meringue pie, use the rind of 1 large lemon instead of the lime rind, or a mixture of finely grated lemon and orange rind, and lemon juice instead of lime juice.

Trifle

SERVES 6-8

6 trifle sponges
4 tbls plum jam
12 ratafia biscuits
50 ml (2 fl oz) orange juice
2 tbls cherry brandy, optional
25 g (1 oz) caster sugar
400 ml (14 fl oz) milk
2 eggs (size 2)
5 ml (1 tsp) vanilla essence
142 ml (5 fl oz) carton double cream,
   whipped
To decorate
crystallized violets
crystallized rose petals

• Left: Lime meringue pie
Right: Trifle

Cut the sponges in half through the middle and spread with the jam. Sandwich together again. Cut into small pieces and arrange in a trifle dish. Scatter the ratafia biscuits over the sponge. Pour over the orange juice and cherry brandy if used.

Place the sugar and milk in a bowl and microwave on **High** for 2 minutes.

Whisk the eggs and vanilla essence together. Pour on the milk, whisking well. Microwave on **High** for 3½-4 minutes. Check and whisk the custard every 30 seconds. Leave to cool and set. Whisk and spoon over sponge base.

Pipe cream on to the custard. Decorate with crystallized violets and roses. Chill slightly before serving.

Marbled pudding

SERVES 4

100 g (4 oz) self-raising flour
1/4 tsp baking powder
100 g (4 oz) soft margarine
100 g (4 oz) caster sugar
2 eggs
1 tbls water
1 tsp vanilla essence
25 g (1 oz) walnuts, finely
    chopped
1 tbls strong cold black coffee

Sift the flour with the baking powder into a mixing bowl. Beat in the margarine, sugar, eggs and water until smooth.

Divide the mixture in half and place in separate bowls. Stir the vanilla essence into one half and the walnuts and coffee into the other.

Drop alternate spoonfuls of the mixtures into a greased 1.2 litre (2 pint) pudding basin. Smooth the surface with a round-bladed knife.

Cover loosely with cling film and microwave on **High** for 4 minutes. Carefully remove the cling film and leave the pudding to stand for 5 minutes before turning out on to a serving plate and serving hot.

Serving idea: Serve with hot pouring custard.
Variations: The marbled effect may be achieved with different colourings, and a variety of flavourings may be used. Half the sponge mixture may be tinted pink with a few drops of red food colouring. Almond essence or grated orange or lemon rind may replace the vanilla essence. For a chocolate flavour, stir 1 tbls cocoa powder mixed smoothly with a little water into half the mixture. Almonds or hazelnuts may be substituted for the walnuts.

Exotic fruit meringue

SERVES 4-6

1 Ogen or Charentais melon
2 kiwi fruit
1 mango
1 banana
2 × 283 g (10 oz) cans lychees,
    drained
2 egg whites (size 2)
100 g (4 oz) caster sugar, plus a little
    extra
To decorate
2 tbls chopped mixed nuts
1 tsp ground cinnamon

Cut the melon in half and remove and discard the seeds. Scoop out the flesh with a baller or teaspoon and place in a bowl.

Peel and slice the kiwi fruit, mango and banana and add to the melon along with the lychees. Mix all the fruits together and divide between 4 or 6 individual dessert bowls. Put the bowls in the refrigerator to chill.

Whisk the egg whites until they form soft peaks. Add half the sugar and whisk until stiff and glossy. Fold in the remaining sugar with a large metal spoon.

Remove the bowls from the refrigerator and cover the fruit in each with the meringue. Sprinkle a little sugar over the top. Microwave on **High** for 2 minutes. Then microwave on **Medium** 3-4 minutes until the meringue holds its shape.

Decorate the meringue with the chopped nuts and cinnamon and serve.

Variations: Other fruits such as pineapple, grapes and peaches may be included. Grated chocolate may be sprinkled on the meringue instead of cinnamon.

● Top: Marbled pudding; Bottom: Exotic fruit meringue

Pineapple upside-down cake

SERVES 4-6

2 tbls soft light brown sugar
439 g (15½ oz) can pineapple rings, drained
glacé cherries
100 g (4 oz) self-raising flour
¼ tsp baking powder
100 g (4 oz) soft margarine
100 g (4 oz) caster sugar
2 eggs
½ tsp vanilla essence
2 tsp water

Sprinkle the brown sugar evenly over a greased 1.2 litre (2 pint) greased microware baking ring.

Arrange the pineapple rings in the base of the ring and place a cherry in the centre of each.

Sift the flour with the baking powder into a mixing bowl. Add the remaining ingredients and beat until smooth.

Carefully spoon the mixture on top of the pineapple rings. Cover loosely with

cling film and microwave on **High** for 6-8 minutes. Remove the cling film.

Leave to stand for 2 minutes, then carefully turn the cake out on to a serving plate.

Serving ideas: Serve for tea or as a dessert, with whipped cream.

Chocolate cake

Makes 8 slices

100 g (4 oz) self-raising flour
25 g (1 oz) cocoa powder
100 g (4 oz) caster sugar
100 g (4 oz) soft margarine
2 eggs
2 tbls milk

Sift the flour into a mixing bowl. Add the remaining ingredients and beat with a wooden spoon until very smooth and thoroughly blended.

Spoon into a 20 cm (8 inch) round microware container. Smooth the surface with a round-bladed knife and cover loosely with cling film.

Microwave on **High** for 5 minutes. Carefully remove the cling film and leave to stand for 5 minutes.

Turn out on to a serving plate and allow to cool completely.

Serving ideas: Split the cake in half and sandwich with chocolate butter cream. Sprinkle the top of the cake with sifted icing sugar.

● **Left: Pineapple upside-down cake**
Right: Chocolate cake

Profiteroles

MAKES ABOUT 20

65 g (2½oz) plain flour
pinch of salt
50 g (2 oz) butter
120 ml (4 fl oz) water
1 tsp sugar
2 eggs
1 egg yolk
For the filling
1 egg white, stiffly whisked
142 ml (5 fl oz) double cream, lightly
*   whipped*
1 tbls caster sugar
For the topping
100 g (4 oz) plain chocolate

Heat the conventional oven to 200°C, 400°F, Gas Mark 6. Sift the flour with the salt onto a plate.

Place the butter and water in a bowl and microwave on **High** for 2½-3 minutes or until boiling.

Stir in the flour all at once and beat with a wooden spoon until the mixture forms a soft ball that leaves the sides of the bowl clean.

Leave for 5 minutes, then beat in the sugar, eggs and egg yolk.

Spoon the pastry into a piping bag and pipe 20 small buns on to 1-2 greased baking sheets. Bake for 25 minutes in the conventional oven, then pierce each bun with a fine skewer to release the steam and allow to cool.

Fold the egg white into the cream with the sugar. Split each bun almost in half and fill them with the cream mixture, using a teaspoon to divide it equally among them.

Place the chocolate in a bowl and microwave on **High** for 1 minute or until melted. Stir until smooth.

Spoon a little melted chocolate over each bun and allow to set. Pile the profiteroles up into a 'pyramid' on a serving platter to serve.

Serving ideas: Serve the profiteroles with chocolate or vanilla ice cream, sweetened whipped cream or chocolate sauce.

Lemon sponge cake

SERVES 6

225 g (8 oz) self-raising flour
¼ tsp baking powder
100 g (4 oz) butter
100 g (4 oz) soft dark brown sugar
2 eggs
2 tsp grated lemon rind
1 tbls milk
2 tsp lemon juice
3 tbls lemon curd (see page 63)
225 g (8 oz) icing sugar, sifted
2 tbls water
yellow food colouring
crystallized lemon slices, to decorate

Grease and line an 18 cm (7 inch) round deep microware container with greased greaseproof paper .

Sift the flour with the baking powder into a mixing bowl. Using the fingertips, rub in the butter, then stir in the sugar.

Beat in the eggs, one at a time, then stir in the lemon rind, milk and lemon juice. Spoon the mixture into the prepared container and cover with cling film. Stand on an upturned plate and microwave on **High** for 2 minutes.

Turn the container and microwave on **High** for a further 2 minutes. Turn again and microwave on **High** for a further 1 minute.

Leave to stand for 5 minutes, then turn out and leave to cool completely.

Split the cake horizontally into 2 layers and sandwich together with the lemon curd. Mix the icing sugar smoothly with the water and food colouring and use to ice the cake. Decorate with lemon slices.

Variation: For an orange sponge, use grated orange rind instead of lemon, orange food colouring and orange buttercream for the filling.

● Top: Profiteroles
Bottom: Lemon sponge cake

Almond roulade

SERVES 6-8
This recipe uses a large square container which cannot be used in a microwave with turntable.

100 g (4 oz) slivered almonds
¾ tsp baking powder
1 tbls melted butter
4 eggs, separated
50 g (2 oz) icing sugar
1 tsp vanilla essence
¼ tsp almond essence
icing sugar, for decoration
For the filling
50 g (2 oz) butter, softened, or soft
   margarine
100 g (4 oz) icing sugar, sifted
1 tbls cocoa powder
1 tsp hot water

Spread the almonds out in a 30 cm (12 inch) square microware Swiss roll container. Microwave on **High** for 5 minutes, stirring twice. Grind the almonds in a blender or food processor. Stir in the baking powder and set aside.

Line the container with greaseproof paper, overlapping the paper to make 'handles'. Brush the paper all over with melted butter.

Place the egg yolks, icing sugar, vanilla and almond essences in a bowl and beat until pale and creamy. Stir in the ground almonds. Whisk the egg whites stiffly, then carefully fold into the yolk mixture, using a large metal spoon.

Spread the mixture evenly in the container and microwave on **High** for 6 minutes. Remove and leave to stand for 1 minute.

Using the paper 'handles', carefully lift the cake out of the container. Place on a wire rack, and cover with a damp tea towel. Leave to cool completely.

Beat together all the filling ingredients. Spread the filling over the cake and roll up carefully like a Swiss roll, using the paper to help you. Sprinkle icing sugar over the top.

Rum and raisin buns

MAKES 24

100 g (4 oz) self-raising flour
¼ tsp baking powder
100 g (4 oz) soft margarine
100 g (4 oz) caster sugar
2 eggs (size 2)
1 tbls water
1 tsp vanilla essence
1 tsp rum essence
50 g (2 oz) raisins

● Left: Almond roulade
Below: Rum and raisin buns

Sift the flour with the baking powder into a mixing bowl. Add all the remaining ingredients and beat until smooth.

Using 2 paper cases for each bun, one inside the other, place 6 double paper cases around the edge of a plate. Put 1 tsp of the cake mixture in each case.

Microwave on **High** for 1½ minutes, rearranging halfway through cooking. Repeat with the remaining mixture. Allow to cool completely.

Serving ideas: The buns may be served plain or iced with a lemon glacé icing.

Fruit scones

MAKES 8

225 g (8 oz) plain flour
pinch of salt
1 tsp bicarbonate of soda
2 tsp cream of tartar
40 g (1½ oz) butter, diced
25 g (1 oz) sugar
50 g (2 oz) sultanas
about 150 ml (¼ pint) milk

Sift the flour with the salt, bicarbonate of soda and cream of tartar into a mixing bowl. Add the butter and rub in with the fingertips until it resembles fine breadcrumbs. Stir in the sugar and sultanas and add enough milk to make a soft dough.

Roll out on a floured surface to about 1 cm (½ inch) thick. Cut into 5 cm (2 inch) rounds.

Place the rounds in a ring on greaseproof paper in the microwave oven, well spaced apart. Microwave on **High** for 3-3½ minutes.

Brown under a hot grill if liked. Allow to cool.

Serving ideas: Serve warm, split and buttered, with honey or jam.

● Fruit scones; Fruit and nut bars

Fruit and nut bars

MAKES 16

50 g (2 oz) margarine or butter
24 marshmallows (1 packet)
100 g (4 oz) crisped rice cereal
75 g (3 oz) dried apricots, chopped
75 g (3 oz) glacé cherries, chopped
50 g (2 oz) chopped mixed nuts

Grease a 30 × 18 cm (12 × 7 inch) Swiss roll container.

Place the margarine and marshmallows in a large bowl and microwave on **High** for 1½ minutes or until melted.

Stir, then quickly stir in the cereal, apricots, cherries and nuts. Press the mixture into the greased container.

Allow to cool completely, then cut into bars.

Serving ideas: These bars make perfect, nutritious additions to children's packed lunches.

Italian tomato sauce

MAKES ABOUT 1.2 litres (2 pints)

900 g (2 lb) Dutch beef tomatoes,
*   skinned and chopped small*
1 onion, finely chopped
1 red pepper, finely chopped
1 clove garlic, crushed
1 tbls brown sugar
2 tbls red wine vinegar
2 tsp paprika pepper
1 tbls fresh chopped basil
salt
2 tbls tomato purée

Put all the ingredients except the tomato purée into a 2½-3 litre (5 pint) casserole dish. Cover and microwave on **High** for 5 minutes. Stir.

Cover and microwave for a further 5 minutes on **High**. Stir in the tomato purée. Cover and microwave for 5 minutes on **High**.

Use for pasta, pizzas etc. To make a thinner sauce, liquidize or sieve.

Hollandaise sauce

MAKES ABOUT 150 ml (¼ pint)

2 egg yolks
1 tbls white wine vinegar
100 g (4 oz) butter, cut into 8 pieces
salt
pinch of cayenne pepper

Prick the egg yolks and place with the vinegar in a small bowl.

Microwave on **High** for 30 seconds. Beat vigorously until smooth.

Beat in the butter, one piece at a time, until the sauce is smooth. Season to taste with salt and cayenne pepper.

Serving idea: Serve with salmon.

Barbecue sauce

MAKES 450 ml (¾ pint)

1 onion, finely chopped
1 tbls oil
150 ml (¼ pint) tomato ketchup
120 ml (4 fl oz) water
4 tbls brown sugar
4 tbls red wine vinegar
3 tbls Worcestershire sauce
3 tbls lemon juice
2 tsp made mustard
salt and pepper

Put all ingredients into a large glass bowl. Microwave on **High** for 5 minutes. Stir.

Microwave, uncovered, on **High** for 10 minutes.

Serving ideas: This sauce goes well with chicken or hamburgers. It can also be served cold at picnics.

Basic Béchamel sauce

MAKES ABOUT 300 ml (½ pint)

300 ml (½ pint) milk
1 small onion, coarsely chopped
1 bay leaf
6 black peppercorns
salt
25 g (1 oz) butter
25 g (1 oz) plain flour

Place the milk, onion, bay leaf, peppercorns and salt in a bowl. Microwave on **High** for 30 seconds. Cover with cling film and leave to stand for 15 minutes. Strain.

Place the butter in a 1.2 litre (2 pint) bowl and microwave on **High** for 30 seconds. Stir in the flour and microwave on **High** for 30 seconds.

Gradually whisk in the milk. Microwave on **High** for 3 minutes, whisking after every 1 minute. Whisk again and season to taste before serving.

Serving ideas: Béchamel is one of the most versatile of sauces:

Cheese sauce, to serve with vegetables and fish: stir in 75 g (3 oz) finely grated mature Cheddar cheese. For a richer sauce beat in 1-2 egg yolks with the Cheddar cheese.

Caper sauce, to serve with roast lamb or grilled lamb chops: add 1 tbls chopped capers.

Mustard sauce, to serve with smoked or pickled fish: add 1 tbls English mustard powder combined with 1 tsp sugar and 1 tbls white wine vinegar.

Parsley sauce, to serve with white fish: add 2 tbls finely chopped fresh parsley.

Prawn sauce, to serve with white fish: add 2 tbls chopped peeled and cooked prawns.

● Italian tomato sauce; Béchamel sauce; Barbecue sauce; Hollandaise sauce

Red berry jam

MAKES ABOUT 750 g (1½ lb)

*450 g (1 lb) mixed red fruits such as
  strawberries, raspberries,
  redcurrants, blackcurrants etc.
1 tbls lemon juice
450 g (1 lb) granulated or preserving
  sugar*

Wash and prepare the fruits. Put into a
2.8 litre (5 pint) glass mixing bowl. Add
the lemon juice.

Microwave on **High** for 5 minutes or
until the fruit is soft. Add the sugar and
stir until dissolved.

Microwave on **High** for 12 minutes
and check for set. If setting point has
not been reached, return to the microwave for a further 2 minutes and check
again. Continue this if necessary until
setting point is reached.

Cool slightly, and then put into clean
warm jars. Cover and label.

Note: Lemon juice helps this soft fruit
jam to set. Pectin or tartaric acid works
in the same way. Blackberries or stoned
damsons may also be included in the
jam.

Serving ideas: Use as a filling for a
sponge cake or jam tarts, or with scones
and whipped cream for a cream tea.

● Red berry jam; Lemon curd;
Chocolate fudge sauce

Lemon curd

MAKES ABOUT 750 g (1½ lb)

juice and rind of 3 lemons
225 g (8 oz) caster sugar
100 g (4 oz) unsalted butter
4 egg yolks

Put the lemon rind, juice and sugar into a large glass bowl and microwave on **High** for 2 minutes.

Add the butter to the lemon syrup and microwave on **High** for 2 minutes. Stir well and leave for 2 minutes.

Beat in the egg yolks using a whisk. Microwave on **High** for 3-4 minutes stirring frequently.

Beat well until mixture is thick. Pour into hot, dry jars. Cover and label.

Serving idea: Use the lemon curd as a Swiss roll filling.

Chocolate fudge sauce

MAKES 300 ml (½ pint)

150 ml (¼ pint) milk
75 g (3 oz) soft light brown sugar
200 g (7 oz) plain chocolate

Place the milk and sugar in a 1.2 litre (2 pint) heat-resistant jug.

Microwave on **High** for 5 minutes. Do not stir. If the mixture boils over, turn to **Low** for a few seconds, then continue cooking on **High**.

Place the chocolate in a bowl and microwave on **High** for 1 minute until melted.

Stir into the milk mixture until thoroughly blended.

Serving ideas: Serve with ice cream or steamed chocolate pudding.

INDEX

Note: this index includes variations suggested in recipes as well as the main recipes.